TRACTORS

100 YEARS OF INNOVATION

TRACTORS

100 YEARS OF INNOVATION

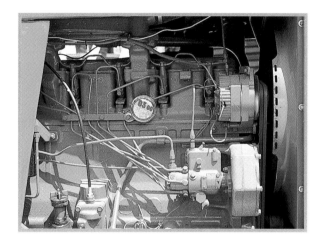

PETER LOVE

LORENZ BOOKS

First published in 2000 by Lorenz Books

© Anness Publishing Limited 2000

Lorenz Books is an imprint of Anness Publishing Limited
Hermes House, 88–89 Blackfriars Road, London SE1 8HA

Published in the USA by Lorenz Books
Anness Publishing Inc., 27 West 20th Street, New York, NY 10011; (800) 354-9657

This edition distributed in Canada by Raincoast Books
8680 Cambie Street, Vancouver, British Columbia V6P 6M9

ISBN 0-7548-0444-5

A CIP catalogue record for this book is available from the British Library

Publisher: Joanna Lorenz
Editor: Debra Mayhew
Designer: Nigel Partridge
Main Photographer: Andrew Morland
Thanks also to Peter Love for photos on pages 8, 9, 10, 12, 25, 38, 46, 47, 51, 52, 53,
58, 59, 60, 61, 63 and 64.
Jacket photography by Andrew Morland. With thanks also to Marc Solvet, France, owner
of the Waterloo Boy.

Printed and bound in Singapore

1 3 5 7 9 10 8 6 4 2

CONTENTS

INTRODUCTION

6 The word tractor has its roots in the Roman Empire when the Latin word *tractorius* was used to describe the act of mechanical pulling. However, it wasn't until the early twentieth century that the internal combustion tractor was capable of pulling farm implements. Since then, the innovative development of tractors has not ceased, and their evolution looks set to continue into the next century. Perhaps, in the not too distant future, a human driver won't be necessary and on farms of more than 600 hectares (1,500 acres) tractors will be controlled from a central farm control centre.

This book shows some of the magnificent old tractors and gives an insight into what they have done for the world economy.

▼ *The horse was "king" on the farm for many centuries and was adapted to many tasks.*

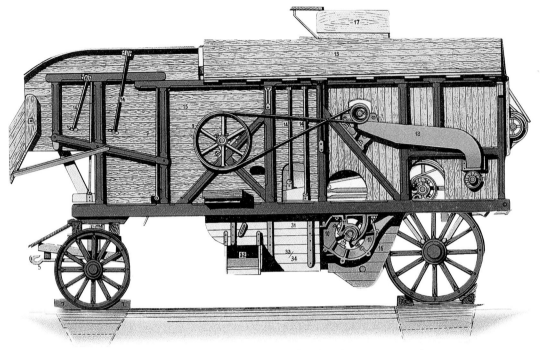

EARLY BRITISH FARM MECHANIZATION

As long ago as 3000 BC, the ox provided the pulling power for the early agricultural societies in the world. Even today some underdeveloped countries still use oxen to plough their land.

In the western world the Agricultural Revolution started in the eighteenth century and continued throughout the Industrial Revolution. One of the first British agriculturalists was Jethro Tull (1674–1741). He invented a wheeled, horse-drawn seed drill and horse-hoe, and in 1733 published a book on his new agricultural methods, *Horse-Hoeing Husbandry*. This caused much controversy in

▲ *The threshing machine became part of farming life for 180 years after its introduction in 1768, until it was finally ousted by the combine harvester.*

its day, but his methods of planting the seed in rows and hoeing the weeds in between formed the basis of all modern agriculture.

Further advances in the mechanization of threshing crops came in 1768, when Scotsman Andrew Meikle invented the first practical threshing machine using a revolving cylinder. In 1812, Cornishman Richard Trevithick advertized the first high-pressure return-flue portable steam engine. This was mounted on

▲ *A two-cylinder Fowler 10 hp ploughing engine working in 1859 at the RASE Warwick meeting. The engine was made by Clayton & Shuttleworth; the ploughing gear came from R Stephenson & Co; the plough came from Ransomes Sims of Ipswich.*

wheels, weighed 5,690 kg (15 cwt) and could be purchased at a price of 60 guineas. This was pulled by horses to wherever it was needed and could drive whatever machine you wanted. In the years after the Napoleonic Wars, however, this great invention fell into

▶ *J & F Howard of Bedford's combined double-drum belt-driven windlass roundabout ploughing tackle, which used one of its portable steam engines to drive the machinery. This method of ploughing was back-breaking and time-consuming.*

▲ *The John Fowler single-cylinder ploughing engine was an amazing worker; the make carried steam ploughing to Egypt, Australia, America, and large areas of Europe. The engine illustrated here is the oldest known example in the world today.*

abeyance. There was very little encouragement for manufacturers to develop such machinery, particularly if it meant the loss of employment on the farm.

The advent of steam power

The Royal Agricultural Society of England was established in 1839 and held its first show in Oxford in the same year, heralding a revived interest in the development of new machinery for farm use. William Howden and Tuxfords, both based in Boston, produced small portable engines. At the next show, in 1841, in Liverpool, England, the famous plough maker J R & A Ransome exhibited a combined engine and thresher, although the design was later discarded. This is considered

▲ *The "father" of the European steam traction engine was Thomas Aveling. Here we see one of his Aveling & Porter 8 hp traction engines, number 2436 of 1889.*

to be the beginning of the modern era of steam portables: by 1850, 5,000 similar engines were at work in the United Kingdom, made by some twenty manufacturers.

Self-moving traction engine

The first self-moving traction engine was introduced in 1849. A two-cylinder under-mounted engine, it was used to drive a threshing machine. Called the *Farmers' Engine*, this machine was produced by E B Wilson of Leeds, and tested by Ransomes & May of Ipswich, Suffolk at various farms in the area. Although it had two gears and the luxury of coil springs on top of the rear axle, this design also had some teething problems. It was not long, however, before Thomas Aveling perfected his hornplate design in 1871 and the British steam traction engine as we know it today was born. By early 1880, Avelings had exported more than 200 traction engines to North America. Of these, number 916 of 1873 still exists in California.

Steam played a large part on British farms, particularly for contract threshing and ploughing until the end of World War II. Today in England there are 2,500 steam engines in preservation and around 3,000 in North America.

GREAT AGRICULTURAL INVENTIONS OF NORTH AMERICA

In 1836, due to depressed working conditions, blacksmith John Deere moved west from Hancock, Vermont to Grand Detour, Illinois. On arrival he found himself in great demand as the village blacksmith.

In early 1837, he was in the local sawmill when he found a broken steel saw blade which he took back to his forge and fashioned into a plough. The area around Grand Detour has rich, black, gumbo soil, characteristic of the prairies, and the early farmers had great difficulty cultivating this soil with traditional ploughs because it stuck to the mould board.

John Deere's polished steel plough sliced through this heavy soil, enabling the pioneer farmers to greatly increase their productivity.

McCormick's reaper

In 1831, Cyrus McCormick of Walnut Grove, Rockbridge County, Virginia, invented and built the first successful reaper. He had spent three years developing this machine to harvest the field crop, and this cut down on the level of intensive labour and drudgery associated with harvesting. The reaper tripled the output of even the most skilful scythe-wielding labourer. At a time when labour was scarce in the Midwest this proved a giant step forward. McCormick spent another three years refining the design before it was patented on June 21, 1834.

In 1840, McCormick went into production with a perfected new machine. The advent of the railways allowed farmers to obtain the machines, even in the most isolated areas. This, coupled with an aggressive advertising campaign, meant that by 1847 McCormick was making 500 reapers a year.

Reaper design was further developed by the Marsh brothers of Delkalb in Illinois when they introduced a binding platform which tied the bundles up, They called this the Marsh Harvester. By 1872, 10,000 of their machines were in service. Self-tying wire binders were introduced later.

This was a boom period. Highly lucrative land deals were offered to settlers by the North American government and more than 600,000 new farms were created. They all wanted new machinery. This growing market saw the beginning of the world dominance of North

▲ *Steam threshing became popular worldwide, although it lasted longer in England than it did in North America. The last of the steam threshing contractors had changed over to tractor power by the end of World War II.*

American manufacturers in agricultural machinery. Companies became larger. William Deering invested in the Marsh Harvester when the company became known as the Deering Harvester Company and in 1902 the McCormick and Deering companies merged to create the agricultural combine International Harvester.

Steam arrives in America

In spite of these developments, the change from horse to steam power was slower in North America than in Britain and Europe. In 1849, one of the first steam engines was produced by the East Coast manufacturer A L Archanbault of Philadelphia. The "Forty-Niner" range was available in various sizes, although North American farmers were slow to take to this new machine and not many were made. The first self-moving engine in the United States was said to have been produced by Obed Hussey of Baltimore Ohio in 1855 and was called a steam plough.

10   Jerome Increase Case was instrumental in introducing steam power to North American agriculture. In 1842, at the age of 22, he left New York to travel to Rochester, Wisconsin, taking with him six brand-new threshing

▲ *The ultimate traction engine to own in North America is the 110 hp J I Case of which there are 12 examples in preservation today. These prairie busters have power steering and can easily pull 8–12 bottom ploughs.*

▼ *The ultimate in steam tractors is this 1924 two-cylinder 20 hp Bryan Harvester Company tractor. Five examples exist in preservation. This is the only Bryan that can be steamed – the boiler runs at 550 psi.*

machines. By the time he reached Rochester, he had sold five. He was a persuasive salesman and did some custom threshing for farmers. He started experimenting to combine the threshing and cleaning operations in one and in 1843 built a new all-in-one threshing machine. He demonstrated this in 1844 at Henry Cady's Cherry Hill Farm. It was very successful but, like those of other manufacturers of the time, it was horse-driven. He eventually set up shop on the Root River.

    In 1862, Case produced a larger Sweepstake range of threshers which could thresh 300 bushels per day. At least eighteen horses were needed to drive one of the large threshing drums so Case started to build a portable engine, introducing the first portable steam engine in 1869. The first self-moving chain-drive engine was produced in 1878 and by 1880 there were 24,000 steam units being used on farms throughout the United States.

    The height of steam power on American farms was 1910, when 72,000 units were in use; by 1930 the number had fallen to 25,000.

The decline of steam power

Steam engines had some disadvantages. To run the engine the farmer needed a crew of two, plus people to supply water and coal.

The threshing machine also required a crew, not forgetting the "cook boy". In the wheat belts of North America and Canada, where farms were often very isolated, labour, coal and water were all scarce.

To compensate for the lack of coal, many traction engines had longer fireboxes for burning straw. Unfortunately, sparks emitted from the chimney could cause a fire, even if a spark arrester was fitted. To stop this, wheat belt engines were often placed a considerable distance from the threshing drum, although this in turn created problems in setting up the belt between engine and drum.

▼ *The International Harvester Company introduced its first tractor in 1906. By 1908 the A and B type 20 hp tractors were in production.*

It was thought that the internal combustion engine would be more efficient in fuel and labour costs than the steam powered versions. Agricultural machinery powered by an internal combustion engine could be an ideal solution.

THE INTERNAL COMBUSTION ENGINE

In the 1860s J J E Lenoir of France patented the first successful gas engine. The basic engine was further developed by Nikolaus August Otto and his partner Eugen Langen. Ten years later, in 1876, the German duo produced the first four-stroke cycle engine, called the Otto Silent. In less than a year, the

▲ *The Ivel tractor, designed by Daniel Albone, was the most significant European tractor introduced between 1902–1914.*

engine found its way to the United States where it was sold through Schleicher, Schumm & Co of Philadelphia.

In 1885, Carl Benz put a slow-running, 700–900 rpm, single-cylinder engine on a three-wheeled chassis, and today is given credit for inventing the petrol-(gas-)engined car. This led to the internal combustion-engined tractor, which soon took over from steam power on farms throughout the world.

THE FIRST TRACTORS
THE BEGINNING

Otto Langen, Hornsby, Froelich, Dan Albone, Herbert Saunderson, Hart-Parr – the names of the pioneers of the turn-of-the-century who have left their mark forever.

By this period, tractors were not only stationary power units to drive the threshing drum, they were actually being used for pulling ploughs and other implements as well, and doing it successfully. The internal combustion engine was not yet quite as reliable as the steam-powered engine, but it was gradually taking over.

Perhaps the most successful pioneer was the company Hart-Parr from Charles City, Iowa. Charles W Hart formed his partnership with Charles H Parr while at the University of Wisconsin. Both men were sound engineers and commercially astute. The first tractor, called naturally enough No 1, was built in 1902 and had a twin-cylinder oil-cooled engine, a feature of Hart-Parr tractors for the next 15 years.

In 1907, Hart-Parr's advertisements began to use the term "tractor" for the first time, and they claimed to have invented the word. As time went by, the word tractor became the standard used by the industry.

In the pages that follow, we look at the most famous early, petrol(gas)-powered tractors. These nostalgic models also serve to highlight the amazing rate of development of the tractor market in the pioneer years.

▲ *An engine detail from a 1918 Fordson Model F tractor, superbly and lovingly restored.*

◄ *Hart-Parr were the leaders in early tractor sales, particularly after the introduction of the 30–60 "Old Reliable". They were the first company to popularize the term "tractor".*

WATERLOO BOY

Made by the Waterloo Gasoline Engine Company, the Waterloo Boy was one of the most important early tractors. Their range started off with the 15 hp L and LA models in 1913–14, and the R model

▼ *The Waterloo Boy was several years in development until it was reliable enough to sell. It was not a large machine, and reflected the need for a tractor that could be adapted to all tasks.*

▲ *The Waterloo Gasoline Engine Company can trace its roots to the 1892 John Froelich machine, which was fitted with a Van Duzen single-cylinder engine and was one of the very first self-moving tractors.*

was introduced on January 26, 1914. This was succeeded by the two-speed N range. In 1918 the John Deere Company took over the Waterloo company in order to enter the tractor market. The N range was kept in production until 1924 when it was replaced by the D range. By then, 20,534 of the N range tractors had been made.

It was at this time that the tractor market became regulated, thanks to the efforts of Wilmot F Crozier, Nebraska's State Legislator, and Senator Charles Warner of Waverly, Nebraska. In July 1919 it became Nebraskan law for every tractor manufacturer to procure

▲ *About 3,000 Model Rs were sold in the United Kingdom under the Overtime banner, along with some 1,000 of the two-speed Model N. The steering was by chain and roller, replaced in 1920 with automotive-type steering.*

Harry Ferguson was the agent in Ireland for John Deere, selling Overtime tractors, and this was the catalyst for Ferguson's interest in tractor design.

a licence issued by the state railway commission for every tractor sold in the state; the only way to gain a licence was to have the tractor tested at Nebraska University. The Nebraska Tractor Tests established the benchmarks for the industry. The John Deere N was the first tractor to be tested at the University of Nebraska in this way. Tested on March 31, 1920, the tractor performed satisfactorily except for the governor action.

JOHN DEERE MODEL N

- YEAR 1919
- ENGINE Two-cylinder 7,620 cc (465 cu in)
- POWER 16 dhp, 25 bhp
- TRANSMISSION Two speed
- WEIGHT 2,800 kg (6,183 lb)

HUBER SUPER-FOUR

16   Huber was one of the many companies that made tractors in the United States between the world wars. The company first attempted to enter the market in 1898 although this was a failure largely due to carburettor problems. A second attempt was made in 1912, then in 1915 the company

▼ Silhouetted against the sky like a relic from a former farming age, the 15–30 Huber Super-Four was introduced in 1921. This tractor was similar in size to the Light-Four but had a larger engine made by Midwest.

produced the 15–30 Huber Super-Four. This tractor was powered by a Sintz Wallen engine, built in Grand Rapids, Michigan, but it too suffered from carburettor problems and its production was discontinued.

The first lightweight tractors made by Huber came out in 1917, beginning with the 12–25 Light-Four. This was fitted with a side-valve Waukesha transverse four-cylinder engine, which had a two-speed gearbox with reverse. Huber never made their own engine, instead preferring to use other manufacturers' proven products. Remarkably, the Light-Four

> **HUBER MANUFACTURING CO**
> **SUPER-FOUR**
>
> • YEAR 1921
> • ENGINE Four cylinder
> • POWER 26 dhp, 44 bhp
> • TRANSMISSION Two speed
> • WEIGHT 2,760 kg (6,090 lb)

stayed in production until 1928. A new Huber Super-Four was introduced in 1921 and was a very powerful tractor.

Huber earned a good, honest reputation. In 1921, when the Super-Four tractor was tested at Nebraska it was found to be under-rated, so in its last year of production, 1925, it was designated the 18–36.

During World War II, Huber concentrated on roller construction. After the war they continued to make industrial equipment, including tractor-based road sweepers, but they never returned to the tractor fold again.

▲ The Super-Four is a more desirable tractor for the collector than the Light-Four, as production of this model ceased in 1925 and fewer were made. The fan belt drove the pulley to keep the engine cool.

◀ The four-cylinder overhead-valve engine used in the Huber Super-Four had a Kingston LD4 magneto and a proven Kingston L carburettor.

ADVANCE-RUMELY 16-30 MODEL H AND 40-60Z

18 **R**umely was set up in 1857 at La Porte, Indiana, who produced farm machinery and steam engines for agricultural use. The President, Dr Edward Rumely, was the third generation of Rumelys. In 1908, John Secor joined the company to develop an oil-fuelled engine that would run on low-grade fuel. Secor perfected a carburettor that ran on both kerosene and paraffin and in 1909, with the help of the factory superintendent, W H Higgins, the first OilPull tractor was built.

In the early years, Rumely concentrated on producing big machines for the large farms on the prairies and produced the popular OilPull range of tractors. The Model B 25–45

▼ *A 1920 16–30 Model H Advance-Rumely was first introduced as a 14–28 in 1917, with a two-cylinder engine. When the 16–30 was tested at Nebraska this tractor set a new efficiency record of 9.94 hp per hour. A new lightweight model was introduced in 1924.*

▲ *Rumely OilPulls are highly sought after in the preservation field, particularly by veteran tractor collectors. OilPulls were never imported into western Europe and only arrived when they were brought in by tractor enthusiasts for preservation.*

was produced in 1910 and lasted until 1912. Also in 1910, the company introduced the two-cylinder 30–60 E, which remained in production until 1923 when it was replaced by the lightweight 30–60 S, which in turn was

ADVANCE-RUMELY THRESHER CO MODEL H

- YEAR 1920
- ENGINE Two cylinder 7 x 8.5 in
- POWER 16 dhp, 30 bhp
- TRANSMISSION Two speed
- WEIGHT 4,308 kg (9,500 lb)

phased out in 1927. The successful OilPull range of tractors was nicknamed the "King of the Prairies". Advance-Rumely entered the small tractor market in 1916 with the All Purpose 8–16 model. In total, 56,500 OilPulls were produced.

Owing to a failed order to Russia, the company hit hard times and in 1931 was taken over by Allis-Chalmers. This gave La Porte a new lease of life, but the works was finally closed in the 1980s. The famous works chimney was pulled down in 1998.

▶ *A beautifully preserved 40–60Z Advance-Rumely showing the giant cooling tower. This model was made only in 1929; 153 tractors were manufactured, though more were produced by converting surplus stock 30–60 S models. This conversion was not a success, so they were converted back again.*

CASE 10-18 CROSSMOTOR, CASE 15-27 & CASE 22-40

20

JI Case and Company was formed in 1863 and became the J I Case Threshing Machine Company in 1880. Today the Case International Harvester Company remains one of the giant international companies in the field of agriculture with a reputation for the high standard of its products.

Case built its first experimental gasoline-powered tractor in 1892. The machine was not a success. Nearly twenty years later, David P Davis developed a two-cylinder range of 40 and 60 machines and the Case 30–60 won first place in the Winnipeg Tractor Trials

▲ *A 10–18 Case Crossmotor built in 1919. Case made 3,515 of this model and still could not keep up with demand. The tractor was capable of pulling a 2-furrow plough or driving a threshing machine.*

▶ *The pulley side of the 22–40 clearly shows what makes this crossmotor tick. A Kingston E carburettor was used for this machine with a Bosch ZR4 magneto. The spark plug leads are very prominent as well. In all, 1,850 of this model had been made when production stopped in 1924.*

of 1911. This then led to the development of four-cylinder tractors and the Case 10–18 Cross-motor was the third generation of these machines. It was derived from the 9–18B. The idea of placing the engine across the frame was for simplicity of layout as well as for ease of maintenance. It was well engineered and used the engine as a load bearer. Case tractors of this period were painted the same as their steam counterparts: sheet metal and castings Brunswick green; wheels red. The cast-iron

The Case 22–40 came out in 1919. The tractor was designed as a four- or five-plough machine, and was successful in coping with this. The 22–40 and the bigger 40–72 did not use the standard Case castbed, but traditional chassis rails.

radiator was black. In many cases the tractor even had detailed lining with the Case name in red and white lettering.

Case was reasonably successful with its crossmotor tractors, which were rather noisy in the gear train. The 15–27 introduced in 1919 was the most successful – in its ten-year run it was re-rated as the 18–32 in 1924 and the K model in 1927. A total of 17,628 of these tractors was made.

CASE CROSSMOTOR 15–27
• YEAR 1919
• ENGINE Four-cylinder 11.5 x 15 cm (4.5 x 6 in)
• POWER 15 dhp, 27 bhp
• TRANSMISSION Two speed
• WEIGHT 2,880 kg (6,350 lb)

▼ *The three-plough 15–27 model was also introduced in 1919 and became a bestseller. In the first year of production 5,522 were made. Many first-time buyers in the United States started off with one of these tractors.*

FORDSON'S MODEL F

22

Henry Ford had always been interested in tractors. He grew up on a farm and ran his own 2,000-acre farm at the same time as working in the motor industry. Setting up a new factory in Dearborn, Michigan, Ford's aim was to adapt the mass-production techniques he had applied to the motor industry to tractor manufacturing.

The Ford Motor Company built their first tractor prototype in 1907. Then, in 1915, Henry Ford announced that he intended to build a "people's tractor". He planned to sell this for less than $250, to do for farming what the Model T Ford had done for motoring. An X-series prototype was shipped to England and tested in January 1917. The trials were a great success and there was a call for the tractor to be built in England. This proved too costly and the Model F went into production in 1917 in the United States and was launched in April 1918 for $750, more than planned but still a good price.

> **FORDSON MODEL F**
> - YEAR 1918–9
> - ENGINE Four-cylinder Hercules 4,113 cc (251 cu in)
> - POWER 20 hp
> - TRANSMISSION Three speed
> - WEIGHT 1,230 kg (2,710 lb)

The secret of the Model F was its stressed cast-iron frame construction that contained all the moving parts encased in dustproof and oil-tight units. This clean-frame construction eliminated many of the weaknesses of the early tractors. The Model F revolutionized farming, bringing the benefits of agricultural mechanization to thousands of farmers all over the world. The Fordson was the best-selling tractor in America for many years. By the time the Ford Motor Company stopped manufacturing tractors in the United States, more than 750,000 had been produced.

◀ *Henry Ford's efforts to call the tractor the Ford tractor had been thwarted by the Ford Tractor Company which had set up using the name of one of its partners. Ford therefore called his tractor the Fordson after the company, Henry Ford & Son.*

▲ *Charles Sorensen was head of Ford's tractor project, and Eugene Farkas was in charge of design. Together they set out to design a mass-produced and affordable "people's tractor". The result was the Fordson Model F which first went on sale in April 1918 and proved to be a great success.*

◄ *The Fordson F was fitted with a Holley carburettor and vaporizer, a side-valve engine and low-tension ignition. The black trembler coil box caused considerable headaches over the years and most Fordsons ended up with a high-tension magneto as fitted on the later models.*

THE TRACTOR TAKES OVER

1920-1939

At the end of World War I, there were around 230 tractor makers around the world; 186 of them in the United States. With the War over these companies could concentrate on developing new designs and world markets.

Many companies experimented with motorized ploughs with varying degrees of success, but many, unfortunately, failed to produce a workable version. One notable success was the Moline Plow Company's Universal two-plough tractor. The innovative design comprized a two-cylinder, front-wheel drive motor unit, with the controls placed well back on the frame. A whole set of specially made implements came with the tractor.

The Depression brought amalgamations within the industry as companies strove to survive. By 1933, production of tractors had dropped from 70,000 a year to 20,000 and by 1939 there were only nine major tractor manufacturers left in the United States and three in England.

The bestselling tractor of the period was the Fordson F. However, even Ford was not exempt from the Depression. For a time the company survived by price cutting but other manufacturers, notably International Harvester, followed suit and the introduction of their Farmall ("farms all") range of tractors saw them take over from Ford as the leading innovators in tractor design and production.

One of the leaders in engine power in the 1920–39 period was International who produced a fine range of over-head valve engines for the Farmall and McCormick-Deering range. However, they fitted a very smooth-running six-cylinder side-valve engine in the W40 series introduced in 1934.

The powerful Allis-Chalmers Model U was an outstanding success over the years of its long production run (1928–1952). There were 19,009 Standard Us made, the example here features French & Hecht wheels.

JOHN DEERE MODEL D – THE "JOHNNY POPPER"

26

John Deere entered the tractor market in the USA with the purchase of the Waterloo Gasoline Engine Company in 1918. The two-cylinder Model D was the first "true" John Deere tractor and was introduced in 1923. The company had been working on a number of versions of the Waterloo Boy range throughout the years 1919–22, called A, B and C. The D prototype, which was the designation given to the production model was Deere's interpretation of the cast-iron frame powered by a two-cylinder engine.

▲ *The 1924 Model D was classed as a three-furrow plough tractor. It was initially available with two speeds and was made in standard form only. A feature of the early Ds was the spoked flywheel which gave this model the nickname of "Spoker D".*

◄ *The first Model Ds had a 65 cm (26 in) flywheel, as illustrated. In 1924, the 60 cm (24 in) flywheel was fitted, of which 4,876 were made, before the company changed to a solid cast-keyed flywheel in 1926.*

The John Deere engineers considered that the post-World War I boom in tractor production was over, and decided to adopt the two-cylinder engine rather than the four- as offering economies of both manufacture and maintenance. This decision was proved to be correct, and this tractor remained in production for the next 30 years, although the performance was continually upgraded during this time. The 1924 model was rated 22–30 hp at the Nebraska Tractor Tests, while the 1953 model achieved 38–42 hp in the same tests.

Deere's decision to manufacture the Model D tractor was a brave one. The tractor was introduced when farming was depressed, however the company's reliable reputation gave the machine a good start. It was relatively expensive to buy at $1,000, but the farmer was buying a durable tractor.

▼ *In 1931 the engine governing speed was increased to 900 rpm and the steering box was changed to the right-hand side. The 1935 tractor shown here had three-speed transmission with a top speed of 6.5 kph (4 mph) and pneumatic tyres were also fitted. This example has French & Hecht wheels.*

▲ *John Deere achieved considerable export sales with the Model D. In 1929 the company sold 2,194 tractors to Argentina and 2,232 to Russia, and Russia purchased more the following year. While the company added other models to its range in the late 1920s and early 1930s, the Model D tractor remained true to its original design.*

JOHN DEERE MODEL D

- YEAR 1935
- ENGINE Two-cylinder 8,210 cc (501 cu in)
- POWER 29 dhp, 37 bhp
- TRANSMISSION Three speed
- WEIGHT 1,997 kg (4,403 lb)

INTERNATIONAL'S FARMALL F-20

28 The International Harvester Company was faced with overwhelming competition from the Fordson at the beginning of the 1920s. International responded vigorously, firstly by giving away a free plough with each of its 10–20 Titan and 8–16 models, known in Europe as the Junior. In 1923, the newly-introduced four-cylinder 10–20 and 15–30 Standard

▼ *Nearly 150,000 F–20 tractors were made before production was phased out in 1940 in favour of the Farmall H. Other tractors in the Farmall range included the smaller, one-plough, F–12 which came out in 1933 and was extremely popular, with 123,442 made. The bigger F–30 had a larger engine which produced 32 bhp, but only 29,526 of these larger tractors were made.*

FARMALL F-20

- YEAR 1934
- ENGINE Four-cylinder 9.5 x 13 cm (3.75 x 5 in)
- POWER 16 dhp, 22 bhp
- TRANSMISSION Four speed
- WEIGHT 2,062 kg (4,545 lb)

the Farmall Regular, did much to maintain the International Harvester company as the leading North American tractor manufacturer for some years. The F–20 was made in both narrow and standard versions. The tractor retained the traditional International grey livery initially but this was replaced by red livery in 1936. Even today the design is a credit to the "Father of the Farmall", Bert R Benjamin.

▲ *The 1932 F–20 tractor had four-speed transmission and was rated 24.13 hp at the belt and 16.12 hp at the drawbar. A new steering mechanism was included.*

tractors gradually gained in popularity and became known as "Old Faithfuls". This increased the pressure on Fordson.

In 1924, International introduced the first proper row-crop tractor, called the Farmall Regular. This basic tractor was redesigned in the 1930s with International creating three models: the F–12, the F–20 and the F–30. Although these tractors were similar, each machine had different capacities. The Farmall row crop tractor took some time to catch on, however, by much persistence it was to become the market leader and was to set the industry standard. The Farmall F–20 was introduced in 1932 and, like its predecessor,

▶ *The Farmall range of tractors were capable of dealing with most light- and medium-weight threshing drums of the time. The F-20 had the belt speed reduced from 690 rpm to 650 rpm to meet the industry standard. The tractor was powerful enough to handle a two-bottom 35 cm (14 in) plough easily.*

OLIVER HART-PARR 70

30

Hart-Parr merged with the Oliver Chilled Plough Works of South Bend, Indiana on April 1, 1929, along with the American Seeding Machine Company and the Nichols & Shepard Threshing Machine Company. They formed the Oliver Farm

▼ *The six-cylinder overhead-valve engine was very powerful for its time and became well liked by farmers. It had a four-speed transmission and a top speed of 9.46 kph (5.88 mph). The striking Brunswick green livery and the red flash bore a passing resemblance to a Ford Model Y car.*

▲ *The 1938 model was restyled with a more streamlined look and a new paint scheme. Oliver was the first company to offer electric lighting as an option on its tractors, and also offered a starter motor and a six-speed gearbox in 1939. The gearbox became standard on all 70 series machines from 1944.*

OLIVER 70

- YEAR 1938
- ENGINE Six-cylinder 3,294 cc (201 cu in)
- POWER 23 dhp, 30 bhp
- TRANSMISSION Four speed
- WEIGHT 1,497 kg (3,300 lb)

Equipment Company with Joseph D Oliver as the chairperson. When Oliver took over Hart-Parr, Oliver had a new tractor on the block, a single-wheeled row crop on high-

▼ *Variations on a theme could be purchased from Oliver. Even today most tractors have individual specifications. This B wide-front Oliver 70 Row Crop, built in 1947, came near the end of Oliver 70 production, which ceased in 1948.*

◄ *An Oliver Hart-Parr 18–27 tractor dating from 1932 but with pneumatic tyre and wheel conversions added later. This tractor remained in production until 1937, when it was replaced by the Model 80.*

clearance tiptoe wheels. This was the basis of the new company tractor. Known as the 18–27, it could be purchased in many forms and was in production from 1931 to 1937. Oliver was the first company to introduce adjustable rear wheels on their row-crop tractors that could be altered to fit the spacing of the crop. This useful invention was soon copied by other tractor manufacturers.

Oliver Hart-Parr introduced the Row Crop 70 HC in October 1935 and this machine proved extremely successful. It had a six-cylinder gasoline high-compression HC engine and was noted as being quiet and smooth-running. More than 5,000 units were sold in the first six months of production, 3,000 more than had been anticipated. In 1937, "Hart-Parr" was dropped from the company name and thereafter the Model 70 Row Crop tractor carried only the Oliver name.

Oliver was bought by the White Motor Corporation in 1960, which merged its agricultural interests under the banner of White Farm Equipment.

JOHN DEERE B SERIES

32

The 1935 John Deere B model evolved from the Model A, which had been introduced in 1934. The Model A was mainly a row-crop tractor, and when it was first introduced it contained a number of innovations. The width of the wheel track was adjustable through the use of splined hubs whilst the transmission was contained in a single-piece casting. Originally the Model A was rated as 18–24 hp but this output was later increased. The Model A remained in production for 18 years and over 328,000 were made.

▶ *When the Model B row-crop range was introduced, it had a power rating of 9–14 hp and a 2,444 cc (149 cu in) engine. The tractor was designed to run on various fuels, depending on the customer's needs.*

▼ *Just over 300,000 Model B tractors were made during the production run that ended in 1952. The 1938 BWH, illustrated here, was a popular model in California and was in production for 18 months before the tractor was restyled.*

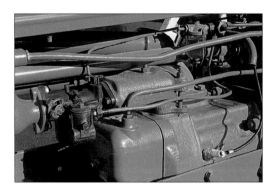

The Model B was designed for the smaller farmer and was initially rated as 9–14 hp although the engine was later upgraded. It was made in 11 configurations, from the tricycle B to the standard BR version and the adjustable wide-front high-clearance BWH. The Model B helped establish John Deere in the forefront of tractor design. The standard two-cylinder Model BR was a popular tractor in England in the late 1930s, although the cost stopped it selling in large quantities.

JOHN DEERE BWH

- YEAR 1937–1938
- ENGINE Two-cylinder 2,442 cc (149 cu in)
- POWER 11 dhp, 16 bhp
- TRANSMISSION Four speed
- WEIGHT 1,485 kg (3,275 lb)

◀ *The Model B series had three significant engine changes during its life, making it more powerful as it progressed, although it always remained a two-cylinder tractor. The most noted modification came with the Henry Dreyfuss styling change in 1938. Then in 1947, a longer frame, six-speed transmission and lights were added.*

▼ *The BO Lindeman was available from 1943–1947. The Lindeman brothers of Yakima, Washington, were exceptionally clever engineers. They had already converted a number of GP models for track-laying purposes in local orchards before the BO Lindeman "official" version was produced in 1943. In December 1946, the Lindeman Power Equipment Co was bought by John Deere. By this time the MC tracklayer was being made at Yakima.*

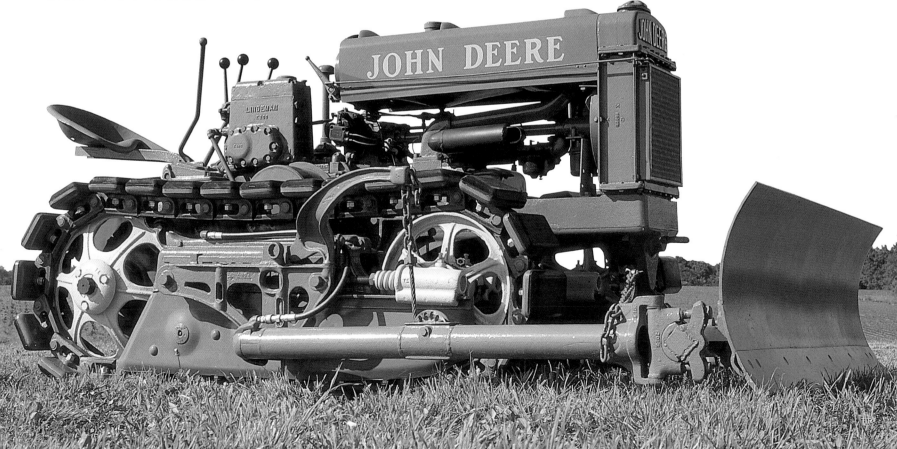

ALLIS-CHALMERS U

The Edward P Allis Company was known for its huge pumping and mill engines. Under General Otto Falk, who became president of the company in 1913, Allis-Chalmers diversified away from heavy industry into lighter products. Farm tractors were just one of the company's new lines.

In 1918, after a number of failed attempts at making a reliable tractor, the 15–30 was introduced. This conventional tractor was a big hit but sales were very slow.

However, the purchase of Advance-Rumely in 1931 gave the company the dealer network it had been looking for. The Model U came

▼ *A 1935 row-crop tractor first produced by Allis-Chalmers in 1929. Originally called the "All-Crop", this tractor later became known as the UC. Even with the ingenious "drive-in" cultivator system introduced by the company, sales of this tractor were not very exciting.*

ALLIS-CHALMERS U

- YEAR 1935
- ENGINE Four-cylinder 4,927.6 cc (300.7 cu in)
- POWER 30 dhp, 34 bhp
- TRANSMISSION Four speed
- WEIGHT 2,332 kg (5,140 lb)

▲ The Model U Allis-Chalmers tractor was first produced in 1929. The Persian Orange colour of these tractors was introduced when Harry Merritt, the Tractor Division manager, visited California in 1929 and saw the wild orange poppies standing out in the fields.

◄ In 1933, the engine was replaced by the Allis overhead-valve unit which produced 34 hp. By this time, pneumatic Firestone tyres were supplied as standard, making the Model U the first tractor in the world to have them. The original is on display at the Wisconsin State Historical Museum.

on the scene in 1929. It had a four-speed transmission and a Continental side-valve engine, replaced in 1932 with Allis-Chalmers' own overhead-valve 34 hp UM engine. Without doubt this was one of the most successful spark-ignition engines ever fitted in a tractor, with an excellent governor to match.

In 1933, Barney Oldfield set a tractor speed record with one of these machines when he lapped a mile course at Dallas, Texas, at an average speed of 103.5 kph (64.28 mph). This speed record was part of the advertising campaign for pneumatic tyres – the U was the first tractor in the world to carry these. It was left to Ab Jenkins to set the final record on Utah Salt Flats at 109.2 kph (67.877 mph).

BRITISH-BUILT FORDSONS

FORD STANDARD MODEL N

- YEAR 1937
- ENGINE Four-cylinder 4,375 cc (267 cu in)
- POWER 26.6 hp
- TRANSMISSION Three speed
- WEIGHT 1,490 kg (3,284 lb)

◄ *In 1937 the Fordson N was offered with either steel or pneumatic tyres and wheels, most wartime tractors had steel wheels as rubber was in short supply.*

▼ *The new orange colour scheme was introduced in 1937, and other changes were made to the tractor, noticeably the square oil-bath air cleaner and the upright exhaust for the agricultural model.*

In 1919, the production of the Fordson F tractor had begun in Cork, Ireland. This was the first time that tractors had been manufactured simultaneously in the United States and Europe. In April 1929, the manufacture of the Fordson tractor was transferred completely to Ireland. In autumn 1932, Ford's tractor production was switched again to Dagenham, Essex, in England. The Ford Dagenham plant had already been operational, building trucks and cars, since November 2, 1931. Production at Dagenham was a great success and was to be the home of the British built Fordson tractor until 1964 when a new factory was built at Basildon.

The Fordson Standard N was the backbone of the British tractor industry in the 1930s and was in production from 1929 until 1945. In 1935, 10,000 of these tractors were produced. By late 1939, production had risen dramatically with 2,000 tractors a month being made and, in November 1943, the Dagenham plants's 100,000th Standard N came off the production line.

The Fordson E27N Major was introduced on March 19, 1945, painted in a blue livery and with a starter motor fitted as standard. Its engine was similar to the Fordson N; as the Standard N's engines wore out, the E27N version was supplied as the replacement. The last E27N Major came off the line on January 17, 1952, and so ended the line of Fordson tractors that went back to 1917. The "New" Major was a completely new concept.

▲ *A 1944 Fordson converted to diesel. Conversions of the Fordson tractor did take place occasionally, particularly with the Perkins Leopard II engine or the Perkins L–4 engine as illustrated here. During World War II, tractors were painted green to make them less visible in the fields.*

▶ *By 1939, Britain had only 55,000 tractors at work; of these 35,000 were Fordsons.*

CATERPILLAR

38 Caterpillar was formed in 1925 by the amalgamation of two companies who competed for more than 25 years before finally merging. Both companies, Daniel Best and Holt Brothers, had fine West Coast of America pedigrees and at the beginning of the 20th century they developed vehicles to cope with the soft soils of California. Holt had taken over Best's company in 1908 but Best's

CATERPILLAR R2

- YEAR 1934–1937
- ENGINE Four-cylinder
- POWER 27 dhp, 32 bhp
- TRANSMISSION Three speed
- WEIGHT 3,366 kg (7,420 lb)

son, C L "Leo" Best, started up on his own in 1910 as the C L Best Gas Traction Company. Both companies made successful crawler tractors. During World War I, much of Holt's production was for the United States Army and was used in Europe, while Best concentrated on developing machines for use on the farm. The companies engaged in bitter rivalry as the patent for crawler tracks was held by Holt. On April 15, 1925, the two companies merged to form the Caterpillar Tractor Company, with C L Best as president.

The new company was a success, initially concentrating on five models taken from the best of the previous ranges. One of the best-known early models was the Caterpillar Twenty, a mid-sized crawler tractor that recorded a pull of 2,754 kg (6,071 lb) at the Nebraska University Tractor Tests. In 1931, Caterpillar was the second North American company to fit a diesel engine in a track-layer with the Diesel Sixty, which later became known as the Sixty-Five.

◄ *Old Caterpillars never die as witnessed by this model. Taken in September 1999 at Rugby, North Dakota, this picture shows a Thirty Five which dates from 1934. A rare machine, the tractor sports engine side covers which are rarely seen on old "Cats".*

▼ *The Caterpillar R2 had an overhead-valve four-cylinder engine. Only 83 of this model were produced between 1934 and 1937, and they were mostly used on small farms.*

◄ *The R2 differed little from the 2F Twenty-Two. Both were fitted with the reliable Eisemann magneto. The more successful of the two, the Twenty-Two, was manufactured at the same time as the R2 and would stay in production until 1939.*

THE POST-WAR YEARS

1940-1950

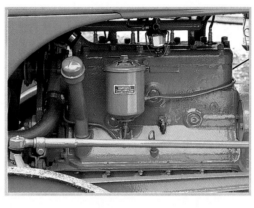

Tractor evolution during the years of World War II and its immediate aftermath is inextricably linked with Harry Ferguson who was the dominant influence on tractor design and innovation during this period. Harry Ferguson was born in 1884, the son of an Irish farmer. He was a brilliant engineer and his involvement with tractors started in his early twenties when he became Belfast agent for Overtime tractors, Waterloo Boy models renamed for the British market.

Harry Ferguson's first tractor was built in 1933 and incorporated his hydraulic draft control and three-point linkage system. After looking round for a manufacturer to build his tractor, David Brown agreed to set up a company and produce these tractors. By May 1936 the first tractor from the Ferguson-Brown Company came off the line. This tractor was called the Ferguson-Brown Model A and 1,351 were made. The partnership was not a success. Harry Ferguson and David Brown argued over the direction the development of the tractors should take and in 1939 went their separate ways.

THE "HANDSHAKE" AGREEMENT

In 1938 Harry Ferguson travelled to North America to find a new partner to use his hydraulic system and three-point linkage. His work impressed Henry Ford and together they struck the famous gentleman's agreement. Ford-Ferguson was born.

▲ *Time was tight for the Ford design team working on the N series. The team decided to use the side-valve Ford mercury V8 engine which was cut in two. This formed a successful four-cylinder 1,966 cc (120 cu in) engine.*

◄ *Lanz Bulldog tractors were popular between the World Wars. The single-cylinder hot-bulb semi-diesel Lanz tractor was rugged and indestructible. They were popular all over the world, including Australia and New Zealand. A number of companies built the tractors under licence including Le Percheron, HSCS, and KL Bulldog.*

FORD-FERGUSON N SERIES

The 1939 Ford-Ferguson 9N is without doubt one of the most desirable tractors for American collectors to own. Due to a tooling problem, the first 700–800 tractors off the production line had aluminium grilles and bonnets. However, these were not very durable and many were replaced by pressed steel examples after only a short time in service. This means that, metaphorically speaking, a model with aluminium grilles and bonnets (hoods) is worth its weight in gold to the interested collector.

▼ *The main selling point of the Ford 9N was the Ferguson draft system which revolutionized small-scale farming. Over 99,000 9Ns were produced between 1939 and 1942. The 9N was succeeded by the Ford 2N; nearly 200,000 were produced.*

FORD 8N

- YEAR 1948
- ENGINE Four-cylinder 1,961.5 cc (119.7 cu in)
- POWER 21 dhp, 26 bhp
- TRANSMISSION Four speed
- WEIGHT 1,093 kg (2,410 lb)

▶ *The 8N was developed from the 2N. Production on this model started in 1947, and it was a great success. More than 52,000 8Ns were produced, with production finishing in 1952 when the NAN series took over.*

▼ *Many of the internal components of the engine, including the pistons, were compatible with the Ford V8 automobile in production at that time.*

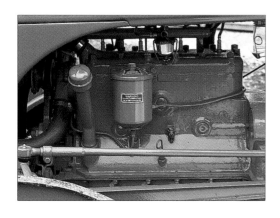

The Model 9N is one of the most famous tractors ever produced and was the first to incorporate the Ferguson draft control system. This tractor was first demonstrated in the town of Dearborn, Michigan on 29th June, 1939.

The 9N was developed as a versatile all-purpose tractor for the small farm and met its objectives very well. The engine used was produced from half a Ford Mercury V8 engine, which created a four-cylinder side-valve 1,966 cc (120 cu in) engine. For the North American market the tractor ran on petrol (gasoline) predominantly, although some ran through a Holley 295 vaporizing unit using distillate fuel. These were designated the 9NA, and the majority of these 21 hp tractors were delivered to Britain.

The 9N was in production until 1942 when the utility 2N was introduced, owing to wartime shortages. The 8N was introduced in 1947 and was in production until 1952.

FERGUSON TE20 SERIES

44

After unsuccessfully trying to persuade Ford to produce the N series tractors in England, Harry Ferguson returned to Europe and set up a deal with Sir John Black of the Standard Motor Company. Premises were found at Banner Lane, Coventry, where Massey-Ferguson tractors are still made today.

The first Ferguson came off the line on July 6, 1946. It was similar to the Ford-Ferguson series tractor, but had a more powerful 24 hp Continental Z-120 engine and

---

FERGUSON TEF

- YEAR 1956
- ENGINE Four-cylinder diesel 2,092.3 cc (127.68 cu in)
- POWER 25 bhp
- TRANSMISSION Four speed
- WEIGHT 1,225 kg (2,700 lb)

four gears. The tractor was to be produced in a full range of models, including the TE series, which stood for Tractor England, and the TO: Tractor Overseas. The TO tractor was hugely popular. Over 500,000 were built in Coventry, England between 1946 and 1956, and some 60,000 TO20 "Fergys" were built in North

◄ *The TE20 had a 24 hp Continental Z-120 four-cylinder engine with a four-speed gearbox. The three-point linkage and draft system patented by Harry Ferguson went straight on the back.*

▲ *In many respects the TE20 was virtually a copy of the Ford 9N. Nevertheless it was an instant success, particularly in Europe and the British colonies.*

America from 1948 to 1951. This tractor inspired great affection and appeared on many British farms. It is still much in demand by enthusiasts, and a large number can still be found at work in the fields some 50 years later. Such longevity says much for the quality and the standard of the engineering of the post-war period.

In 1953, Harry Ferguson sold the company to Massey-Harris. The grey Ferguson was phased out in 1956 and in 1957 its derivative, the FE35, was introduced. In 1958 the livery and name was changed to Massey-Ferguson.

▲ *The three-point linkage required a full Ferguson system of implements that was very extensive indeed; some of these were not made by Ferguson but were subcontracted.*

▼ *Diesel power was slow to affect the Ferguson tractor. Eventually Perkins offered the P3 conversion for the tractor. A four-cylinder diesel engine came out in 1951.*

ALLIS-CHALMERS B

Allis-Chalmers entered the small farm tractor market with the Model B in 1937 which cost $495 to buy. It had pneumatic tyres and was an instant success. During a lengthy production run, between 1937 and 1957, more than 120,000 were produced.

The success of the Allis-Chalmers Model B tractor owed much to the introduction of pneumatic tyres offered with this tractor from

▼ *The first 96 B tractors made used the Waukesha FCL engine. In 1938, Allis introduced its own more powerful four-cylinder 16 bhp overhead-valve engine. The bore of the engine was increased in 1943.*

▶ *A 1941 Allis-Chalmers B tractor showing the stylish bonnet (hood) and grille fittings. These were introduced by the industrial designer Brooks Stevens.*

ALLIS-CHALMERS B

- YEAR 1948
- ENGINE Four-cylinder 2,048 kg (125 cu in)
- POWER 20 dhp, 22 bhp
- TRANSMISSION Three speed
- WEIGHT 997 kg (2,199 lb)

The Allis Chalmers Model B is a popular tractor on the preservation scene. This 1948 British-built example was photographed on display at a rally near Edinburgh, Scotland.

This 1940 North American-built, wide-axle example is seen at a tractor charity road run. Because of its light weight, the Model B is easy to transport to events such as these.

the start. Allis had also taken the step of employing Brooks Stevens of Milwaukee to restyle their tractor range. The style he created for the B was translated to other Allis models, and gave the Allis tractors a family look for the next 20 years.

A good number of the Allis-Chalmers B tractors were exported, and 2,000 skid units were imported into Britain just after the war.

Allis established a new assembly plant at Totton, Hampshire to assemble these tractors, and later moved to a new factory at Essendine, Lincolnshire, where the British B was made until 1954. This was succeeded in production by the D270. However, tractor manufacture in the UK was not successful for Allis, and the company ceased making tractors there in 1968.

LANZ BULLDOG

Heinrich Lanz established his company in Mannheim, Germany, in 1859. He was the German agent for Clayton & Shuttleworth and, in 1863, started distributing McCormick reapers in Germany. This lead him to manufacturing his own farm products, including steam engines.

The company is best known for the Bulldog tractors, which were popular in Europe between the world wars. Bulldogs could run on very low-grade fuel – used engine oil thinned with paraffin, which meant cheap running costs. This was a considerable selling point at the time.

◄ *Lanz Bulldog tractors have been popular in Europe for many years. The Lanz Company was taken over by John Deere in 1956. This is a Lanz D9506 from the range introduced in 1951.*

LANZ 8532 TRAFFIC BULLDOG
- YEAR 1948
- ENGINE Single-cylinder 10.3 litres
- POWER 35 hp
- TRANSMISSION Six speed
- WEIGHT 3,177 kg (7,005 lb)

▲ *Lanz has a big following in the tractor-preservation world and is the number-one company in Central Europe.*

▼ *A D7506 Lanz produced in 1950. During World War II, the Lanz factory at Mannheim was destroyed by allied bombing and so it wasn't until 1948 that Lanz started producing their 35 hp tractor. By 1950, the company could once again offer a full range.*

▲ *The six-speed Lanz HN3 D7506 25 hp all-purpose tractor was a popular medium-sized machine. It was developed not long before World War II and in 1950 cost 150 DM to buy. The tractor went out of production in 1952 when a new range of Bulldogs was on the horizon.*

Although the company made some tractors just before and during World War I, it was in 1921 that the little hopper-cooled, single-cylinder, 12hp HL 6–L engine, hot-bulb tractor came along. The tractor was very simple and reliable, and became extremely popular. The initial Bulldogs were crude. The HL model had no reverse gear, and the engine had to be stalled and then run backwards to enable the machine to be reversed. However, the HL model was gradually improved and the upgraded model became the HR2 in 1926. The principles of the design remained in production until 1960.

THE DEVELOPMENT OF THE MODERN TRACTOR

1950-2000

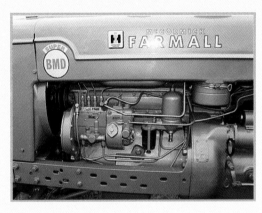

For many people the 1950s were the golden era of tractor design. There were a number of significant developments. Diesel engines became the norm, especially in Europe. Tractors such as the Fordson Major E27N were offered with a diesel alternative and a Perkins P3 diesel engine was also fitted to the Ferguson TE range. Joining in, Case introduced their own six-cylinder Lanova diesel engine in 1952. Case followed up this success a year later with a new model called the 500 which had 56 drawbar horsepower.

The next development was the introduction by International in 1954 of the first "live" PTO, followed later the same year by the "Torque Amplifier" system. In simple terms, this consisted of a hand lever connected to a planetary gear system which doubled the standard five-speed transmission to ten speeds. The design team at Case's answer to this development was the Case-O-Matic, a torque converter ahead of the ordinary transmission that could be locked in or out.

FOUR-WHEEL DRIVE

In Europe four-wheel drive tractors were seen as the way forward. In Germany, MAN made an interesting and successful range and Britain's Roadless and County did the same. In 1960 John Deere produced a monster four-wheel drive, "pivot", two-chassis tractor called the 810.

▲ *Diesel power became very popular in the 1950s. International Harvester Company painted 53 of their Farmall Super BMD tractors in a gold livery to commemorate the Coronation of HRH Queen Elizabeth II.*

◀ *The Massey-Ferguson 95 diesel was a popular tractor in Canada and many of them have lasted in preservation, with a number restored in England.*

MASSEY-HARRIS 745S

Massey-Harris was formed in 1891 in Toronto, Canada from the merger of two farm-implement manufacturers. In the 1930s, the Massey-Harris Pacemaker was popular, and it was during this time that the company chose the famous red and straw colours for their machinery.

The best-known Massey-Harris tractor was the Pony, although this small tractor was more popular in Europe than America where it was considered too small for the larger-sized farms. Around 90,000 Ponys were manufactured at the Massey-Harris factory in France.

▼ *This tractor worked at the Newcastle University farm at Nafferton before being acquired by a Northumberland farmer, the late Eddie Brown. In a poor state of repair this 745S, number N445T, came up at auction in the mid-1980s.*

In 1948, Massey-Harris started production in Manchester, England, with its Model 7 (744). Later, production was switched to Kilmarnock in Scotland where the plant assembled combines and tractors.

It was found that the British Perkins P6 TA six-cylinder diesel engine would fit the North American Model 44 frame, introduced in 1946. About 12,000 744 models were made. In 1954, the 745 was introduced with full hydraulics. Even fewer were produced.

▲ *The actual date of manufacture of this 745S, number N445T, is not known. However, production of this model stopped in 1958, and it is quite possible that it was laid up at the factory for some time in an unfinished state. It has Fordson E27N wheels bolted to Massey-Harris rear centres. The tin work is much thinner than earlier British-built Massey-Harris tractors.*

▲ *A Kilmarnock-built 745S, one of the last in the line for British-made Massey-Harris tractors. This tractor has recently been restored and is one of only three examples in existence in the UK.*

Massey Harris gained a contract to supply tractors for the infamous Ground Nut scheme in Africa, sponsored by the British government. The 745 was the tractor chosen for this contract, with the Perkins four-cylinder L4 TA engine and full hydraulics. About 6,000 of these tractors were made before production halted in 1958.

MASSEY-HARRIS 745S
- YEAR 1958
- ENGINE Perkins L4
- POWER 50 bhp
- TRANSMISSION Five speed
- WEIGHT 2,495 kg (5,500 lb)

DEUTZ D50

At the turn of the century the German company, Deutz, was a well-respected stationary-engine maker. The company was closely involved with the pioneering engine designs of Nikolas Otto. Deutz produced its first tractor in 1907. This was manufactured by its American subsidiary, the Otto Gas Engine Co, but World War I stopped most production. The only exception was the manufacture of some 100 large, heavy artillery tractors.

In 1926 Deutz produced a Lanz look-alike, the MTH 222. This was one of the first diesel tractors made, and instigated diesel tractor technology. In the 1930s, Deutz produced a range of Stalschlepper "Iron Tractor" models

▼ *Deutz company tractors were popular in post-war Europe, particularly the single-cylinder variants. This 1964 multi-cylindered D80 had power steering as a standard feature. The D80 was first made in 1960.*

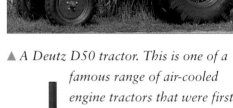

▲ *A Deutz D50 tractor. This is one of a famous range of air-cooled engine tractors that were first introduced by Deutz in 1942.*

▲ *A beautifully preserved 1963 Deutz D25S with an air-cooled two-cylinder 1700 cc (104 cu in) engine.*

including the F1M 414, F2M 317 and F3M 315 with single, twin and three-cylinder engines respectively. Over the years, Deutz supplied a range of engines to other German tractor manufacturers. Their famous range of air-cooled engines began in 1942.

DEUTZ D50

- YEAR 1958
- ENGINE Four-cylinder air-cooled
- POWER 55 hp
- TRANSMISSION Eight forward, four reverse
- WEIGHT 2,606 kg (5,746 lb)

After World War II, Deutz became Klockner-Humbolt-Deutz AG and designed an air-cooled range of diesel tractors. Deutz was one of the first companies to succeed in exporting tractors to the United States. In 1968–1969, the Deutz tractor division merged with tractor and implement manufacturer, Fahr, a company that began life as a reaper manufacturer a few years before World War I. The joint tractor range became known as Deutz-Fahr. In 1985 Deutz bought Allis-Chalmers and formed Deutz-Allis. The company later became part of AGCO.

◄ *In 1990, the Deutz-Allis tractor division was sold to the AGCO Corporation, which still makes Allis tractors today. In 1995, the Italian SAME group purchased Deutz-Fahr; this company, too, still makes a fine range of tractors.*

MASSEY-FERGUSON SUPER 95

Produced in 1958, the Massey-Ferguson Super 95 was very much a stopgap while the merger between Massey-Harris and Ferguson tractors was put into place.

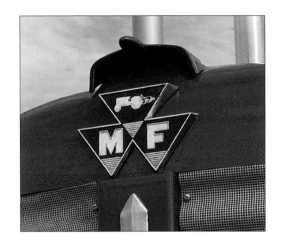

▼ *Acquired by Massey-Ferguson, the Minneapolis-Moline six-cylinder 6,962 cc (425 cu in) engine held its own very well against its rivals. Although a powerful tractor, the design was rather old-fashioned even in 1958.*

◀ *The Massey-Ferguson Super 95 was a redesigned version of the Minneapolis-Moline "Prairie Gold", fitted with a new bonnet (hood) and grille to a Massey design, and painted in the Massey-Ferguson red and silver grey livery.*

Harry Ferguson sold Ferguson tractors to Massey-Harris in 1953, but it was not until 1958 that the name and colour scheme for the Massey-Ferguson tractors were unified.

Both companies had firm adherents in the market place among customers and dealers. Indeed, the MH50 and Ferguson 40 tractors had different bodywork but, mechanically, they were identical as both were based on the Ferguson TO35.

Massey-Ferguson produced its first red and grey tractor in November 1958. This was called the Model MF35 and was powered by

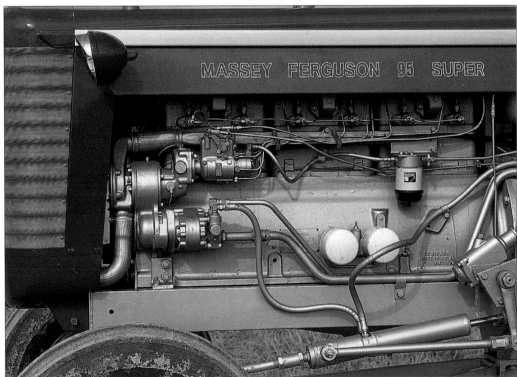

MASSEY-FERGUSON 95

- YEAR 1958
- ENGINE Six-cylinder 6,962 cc (425 cu in) diesel
- POWER 63 bhp 44 dhp
- TRANSMISSION Five speed
- WEIGHT 3,405 kg (7,506 lb)

Perkins engines. The company inherited and then developed a successful range of small- and medium-sized tractors. By the late 1950s, however, farmers were changing to larger, more powerful, models, particularly for the larger ploughs entering the market. In order to counter this trend, Massey-Ferguson began to look at other manufacturers to see if they had a tractor that would fit their own range and provide them with an instant solution. The company discovered that Minneapolis-Moline had the ideal machine.

The Minneapolis-Moline GBD had been in production since 1953, but by the late 1950s the company had fallen on hard times and the prospect of extra sales was not to be dismissed. The six-cylinder 6,962 cc (425 cu in) engine held its own against its rivals and was designed with three individual blocks and cylinder heads. The tractor was slightly old-fashioned but served its purpose. During its three year production run, from 1958 to 1961, 3,025 tractors were sold.

◀ *The Massey-Ferguson Super 95 was not sold in the United Kingdom, although some have now been imported by preservation enthusiasts. In 1961, it was superseded by the more powerful 97. This was offered as a four-wheel drive machine.*

JOHN DEERE 5010

Since 1923, when John Deere produced its first "in-house" tractor design, the two-cylinder engine had been fitted to 98 per cent of all its tractors. But times were changing and the Model 435 of 1959–60, which was very popular in Florida, had a two-cylinder Detroit two-stroke diesel. By 1960, the production lines were all clear for the "New Generation" tractors to be introduced.

In 1953, John Deere started to design a range of multi-cylindered tractors to replace the ageless two-cylinder configuration. The new generation of John Deere tractors took a

▲ *These monster tractors had to be mounted from the rear, with their 62–81 cm (24½–32 in) tyres jutting out from the back. The John Deere 5010 initiated the Category 3 three-point hitch for working with seven-furrow ploughs, like the F245H model, which also utilized the Category 2/3 Quik-Coupler.*

▶ *This 1964 John Deere 5010 is pictured standing in a scrapyard near Drake, North Dakota in September 1999, awaiting a new owner.*

long time to produce, and it was not until 1960 that the company launched its new range, which was designed to meet the demand for larger, more powerful machines. These tractors were first shown in public at Dallas, Texas on August 30, 1960. The four models released in 1960 were the four-cylinder 1010, the 2010, the 3010, and the six-cylinder 4010. The 4010 produced 84 hp and was made for the big-acreage farmer.

This range performed as well as it looked, and set industry standards that John Deere's competitors had to follow. In 1963, the company produced the biggest tractor yet. The 5010 model was the world's first 100 hp, two-wheel drive tractor. The 5010 was sold from 1963 to 1965 with 5,463 agricultural versions being made as well as 2,007 yellow industrial-style models.

JOHN DEERE 5010

- YEAR 1963
- ENGINE Six-cylinder 8,702 cc (531 cu in)
- POWER 109 bhp hp, 109 hp
- TRANSMISSION Eight Syncro-range, three reverse
- WEIGHT 7,258 kg (16,000 lb)

▲ All the new John Deere tractors were designed with a better power-to-weight ratio to increase productivity. Many of these 5010 tractors have been re-engined and fitted with a turbo-charger, which has kept them at work for over 35 years.

◄ The 5010 was designed by the Dreyfuss design team and won instant acclaim for its engine's smooth, sleek lines.

DAVID BROWN'S JUBILEE TRACTOR

60

David Brown only began manufacturing tractors when Harry Ferguson came to him with his innovative design for the hydraulic lift. Only 1,350 of the Ferguson-Brown tractors were produced, and the two

▶ *On May 9 1999, the 60th anniversary of the first VAK–1 was celebrated by the Hampshire branch of the David Brown Club. Over 70 examples attended from all over the UK, including Simon Carr's 1944 VAK–1, shown here. Later in the year a re-enactment took place of the first tractor leaving the works at the Meltham factory.*

◀ *In 1977, David Brown produced its 500,000th tractor. This was a 1412 Hydra-shift model, number 11202707, which became known as the Queen's Silver Jubilee Tractor.*

men parted company in 1939. This split was brought about because Brown wanted to increase the power of the tractor while Ferguson wanted to reduce the cost.

DAVID BROWN 1412

- YEAR 1977
- ENGINE Four-cylinder-turbo 3,594 cc (219 cu in)
- POWER 81 PTO hp, 91 hp
- TRANSMISSION Hydra-shift, twelve forward, four reverse
- WEIGHT 3,463 kg (7,635 lb)

▲ *In 1977, Her Majesty Queen Elizabeth II celebrated her Silver Jubilee. David Brown auctioned its 500,000th tractor at the Royal Smithfield Show in aid of the Jubilee Fund. The tractor sold for £16,000; the normal price was £6,000. The presentation was made by H M Queen Elizabeth II and the Queen Mother. This tractor now belongs to Somerset farmer, Patrick Palmer, and has been restored to a high standard.*

David Brown Tractors of Huddersfield, Yorkshire, then introduced its own design, the VAK–1, at the Royal Agricultural Show at Windsor in 1939. The new tractor featured a hydraulic lift, and over 3,000 orders were taken at the show. Production was hindered by the war but 5,350 had been made by 1945.

After the war, the company reintroduced the VAK–1 in a slightly improved form until it launched its Cropmaster in 1947. This was

followed by a small rear-engined tractor called the 2D. This was similar to the Allis Chalmers G and was designed for the small-scale farmer. The styling of David Brown tractors remained based on the rounded form of the VAK series until 1956, when the company introduced the 900 series, which was followed by the 950. Smaller models, the 850 and three-cylinder diesel 770, were also available. In 1972, the Brown Company was taken over by Case.

NEW HOLLAND

The story of New Holland is a chronicle of 20th-century mergers as companies expanded their agricultural interests and sought additional market share. The story starts with the founding in 1895 of the New Holland Machine Company in Pennsylvania.

Specializing in agricultural machinery, the company changed owners in 1940 and began the production of the first successful automatic hay balers. In 1947, however, the Sperry Corporation acquired the company to form Sperry New Holland, based in Pennsylvania.

▼ *A 1996 Ford New Holland 7840 coupled to a Westmac mower with Glastonbury Tor, Somerset, England in the background. This series of tractors incorporated the modern tractor technology with four-wheel drive and ergonomically designed cabs.*

▲ As the century came to a close, larger and more powerful tractors were the way forward – although perhaps not as large as these dinosaurs. The ultimate New Holland tractor for the 1990s has to be the Canadian Winnipeg-built 80 articulated series and its derivatives; the largest produces 425 hp (855 cu in) from its Cummins N14 six-cylinder turbo after-cooled engine.

▶ On May 16, 1999, New Holland purchased Case-International Harvester for $4.3 billion. This makes New Holland a powerful world player in the tractor market.

FORD NEW HOLLAND 7840

- YEAR 1997
- ENGINE Six-cylinder non-turbo 6,571 cc (401 cu in)
- POWER 90 PTO hp, 100 hp
- TRANSMISSION 16 x 16; other options available
- WEIGHT 4,657 kg (10,267 lb)

In 1986, Ford bought Sperry New Holland and merged it with Ford Tractor Operations, renaming the company Ford New Holland. A year later, this new company acquired a Canadian prairie-tractor manufacturer: Versatile of Winnipeg, Manitoba.

By the late 1980s, Ford Tractor Operations represented just 3.5 per cent of company products and Ford decided that it was time to concentrate on other areas of the business. In 1991, Fiat purchased 80 per cent of the Ford tractor stock, increasing this by another eight per cent in 1992. By 1993 they had bought the whole company and then merged it with FiatGeotech. They renamed the company New Holland. One sad result of this chronicle of mergers is that by the end of the year 2000 the famous Ford name will vanish from tractors completely.

INDEX

With thanks to John Caldwell, Rory Day, William Day,
Jim Espin, Stuart Gibbard, Doctor Nigel Haig, Peter J Longfoot,
Jayne Love, W S Love, Rob Rushen-Smith, Frank Summerlin,
Jim Thomas, Arthur and Simon Tingley, Alan Ward, Phil Weeden
and particularly to Richard Wade.